Landscape Plants

Learn how to grow your own landscape plants from scratch.

Save hundreds of dollars. Simple, easy techniques that work!

You can have a beautiful landscape without spending a fortune.

"Free Landscape Plants"

by Michael J. McGroarty

Leprechaun Press
Perry, Ohio

FREE LANDSCAPE PLANTS
by Michael J. McGroarty

Printed 1996

Leprechaun Press
4390 Middle Ridge Rd.
Perry, Ohio 44081

Printed in the United States of America
Library of Congress Catalog Card Number 95-95170

International Standard Book Number
0-9649563-0-6

Table of Contents

This book is dedicated to my father. He taught me the importance of hard work, the value of knowledge, the therapy of laughter, and a deep appreciation of nature.

A message from the author . . .

I would like to sincerely thank you for purchasing this book. I never thought in a million years that people would pay to read something I had written.

Growing your own landscape plants from scratch is much easier than you might think. Many of the techniques that you will learn in this book are so simple that young children can do them. And with great success I might add!

Finding a beautiful landscape plant and being able to reproduce that plant as many times as your heart desires is not only fun and exciting, but can result in a tremendous amount of savings and or earnings.

I first became acquainted with landscape plants as a high school student working afternoons, evenings, and weekends at one of the larger wholesale nurseries in the community, often putting in 40-50 hours per week while still in high school. At that time I had no interest in landscape plants. It was just a job, but I was delighted to have it. Who wouldn't have been delighted? I was earning $1.60 per hour!

As I laboriously planted, weeded, watered, potted, carried, pruned, loaded, counted, packaged, tied, and dug landscape plants, I slowly learned their common names, botanical names, and many of their unique characteristics. I still did not have much interest in landscape plants, but I was becoming somewhat of an unwilling expert.

After high school graduation I went to work for a landscape contractor whom I had met at the nursery. I wasn't anymore interested in landscaping than I had been in landscape plants, but he had quite a bit of equipment, and I wanted to learn how to operate heavy equipment.

After a few weeks something strange began to happen. I actually started to enjoy landscaping. It was most satisfying to see the plants that I had been working with for so long being artistically placed around peoples homes. I also realized that I knew more about landscape plants than my boss did. I figured if he could landscape peoples homes with his limited knowledge of plants, then so could I.

With that a career was born. I have slowly, but surely, developed a lifetime love affair with landscape plants. Landscape plants have been part of my daily life for the past twenty three years, they have put food on the table and tennis shoes on the kids. Working in the landscape/nursery industry has been quite rewarding for me.

It is my sincere hope that through the pages of this book, you too will learn and develop a hobby that will bring you just as many rewards, and just as much enjoyment.

Once again, thank you for purchasing this book. I realize that as publications go, this book is not perfect. I did not have the financial backing of a large publishing company to aid me with this project. All of the expense involved in bringing this book from the idea stage to your personal library must be incurred by me.

That's why I sincerely appreciate the fact that you traded your hard earned money for a copy of my book. That means a lot to me.

Sincerely,

Michael J. McGroarty

The most important acknowledgment. . .

I would like to extend a heartfelt thanks to my lovely wife Pam. She has made me look good for years. Along with a few million other duties she has, she takes care of our yard at home. People constantly compliment me on how nice our yard looks. I always tell them the same thing; "Thank you, I'll tell Pam what you said, she takes care of the yard." Pam enjoys a nice yard, and she keeps ours just beautiful.

Despite the thousands of hours she has spent weeding, watering, potting, trimming, making cuttings, sticking cuttings, planting liners, planting ground covers, mulching, and performing a number of other difficult tasks, her heart is not in the nursery or landscaping business. She only does these things to lighten my load. Thank you!

Her niche is being the mom. That is where she excels, and it shows in our two sons. Her efforts have molded them into great kids.

"The McGroarty Family Nursery" is just a small backyard operation that serves many purposes.

I truly enjoy working with the plants. During the winter I spend hours gazing out the dining room window admiring the snow covered plants. Pam thinks I'm nutty.

Everybody from nieces and nephews to Grandma's and Grandpa's have spent some time dabbling in our nursery. In this little nursery our boys have learned work ethics, and the value of a dollar. They have watched cuttings they made with their own two hands develop into beautiful landscape plants.

Landscape gardening is a fun, enjoyable and relaxing hobby. It is a great way to get in touch with nature and relieve some stress at the same time. Get your family involved. They will learn things they can use for the rest of their lives.

Share gardening ideas with your neighbors. Start a neighborhood "**Free Landscape Plants Gardening Club**". You will learn a great deal from each other. Write and tell me about it. I'd love to hear from you. *(Sorry, I don't have time to answer letters personally, but I will address some of them in my quarterly newsletter. I'm busy, busy, busy!)*

Notice

Some landscape plants are patented. That means that they are not to be reproduced without first entering into an agreement with the holder of the patent.

Other landscape plants have their names listed as registered trademarks. Which means that they can not be reproduced and marketed without entering into an agreement with the holder of that trademark.

Patented plants and plants with registered trademarks are labeled as such when you buy them. It is my recommendation that you **not** reproduce these plants at all. There are hundreds if not thousands of varieties of plants that you can do.

For more information about this seek legal advice.

Chapter One

How to Use this Book

There are two sections to this book. In the first section you will learn the many different techniques that can be used to propagate landscape plants. Each technique is described in detail along with information as to which plants can be successfully propagated in this manner. There are both drawings and photographs to help you grasp these techniques.

It is not necessary that you memorize each and every one of these techniques. You can always refer back to them when the time comes for you to get started growing your own landscape plants.

The second section of this book is the **"How to do What"** section. In that section you will find a list of many different landscape plants along with information about propagating each one.

Just look up the plant you would like to propagate and find the recommended method of propagation for that particular plant. Pay close attention to the time of the year suggested for each of the propagating techniques.

For instance, if it's the middle of April and
you want to start some Rhododendron cuttings, you
will learn that April is not the time to do
Rhododendrons. So rather than waste your time
trying something that is not likely to work, put a
reminder note on your calendar to do softwood
Rhododendron cuttings after June first. You can also
do hardwood Rhododendron cuttings after Oct. 30.

At the end of this book you will find a section
titled **"What You Should be Doing Now"**. This
section makes it easy for you to engage in the fun of
growing your own landscape plants when it's
convenient for you.

There is something you can be doing at just
about any time of the year, even if you live in a
northern state like I do. It gets mighty cold here in
Ohio during January and February, but there are still
things you can do in the way of growing your own
landscape plants from scratch. Just check the **"What
You Should be Doing Now"** section at the end of the
book.

Chapter Two

Some Basic Information About Landscape Plants and Propagating Landscape Plants

Landscape gardening can be one of the most fun and rewarding hobbies you can undertake. Being able to grow your own landscape plants from scratch is a valuable skill few people possess.

Some landscape plants are very easy to reproduce while some are more difficult. Some plants can not be grown on their own roots. The desired variety has to be grafted on to the rootstock of another plant, usually a plant in the same family. For instance, Weeping Cherry trees are usually grafted or budded onto a Cherry tree grown from seed.

In some cases plants can be grafted onto the rootstock of an entirely different variety of plant. Lilacs are often budded onto the rootstock of California Privet.

Cotoneaster Apiculata is often grafted or budded onto the stem and rootstock of Paul's Scarlet Hawthorn. In this case the rootstock is grown to a height of about 5 feet. The Cotoneaster is then grafted or budded near the top of the rootstock. This combination creates a very interesting and unique umbrella like effect.

Personally, I don't care much at all for Cotoneaster Apiculata in it's natural state. Despite the beauty of the plant's delicate little pink flowers in the spring, followed by brilliant red berries in the fall, the plant has growing characteristics that make it somewhat undesirable. It grows quite low to the ground and has a very dense and rigid branching habit that traps leaves in the fall. Removing the leaves is time consuming and frustrating. The low branches often layer themselves, sprouting roots and growing into areas that they were not intended to be. (Layering is a method of propagation we will discuss later in this book.) When this plant is grafted onto a stem 5' off the ground, these problems do not occur and the beauty of the plant can be truly appreciated.

Growing landscape plants is not like growing vegetable plants for your garden. Producing landscape plants requires considerably more time, but then again the value of a landscape plant is much higher than that of a vegetable plant. Some landscape plants can be grown to landscape size in a matter of just two years, while others can take up to ten years or more.

You might be thinking to yourself, "I am not going to wait ten years for a landscape plant when I can just drive down the road, plunk fifty bucks down on the counter, take the plant home and plant it."

If you have a noticeable void in the landscaping around your home, then it might not be wise to wait ten years for a particular plant. I wouldn't blame you for buying it instead of growing it yourself.

But what if you needed ten? That's five hundred dollars! Or if your home is located on a large lot and you would like to border the property with a Burning Bush hedge and plant a row of variegated Euonymus in front of the Burning Bush. In that case it would be much to your benefit to wait the three or four years it would take to produce 50, 100, or 200 Burning bush and the same number of variegated Euonymus. Especially when Burning Bush often retail for $19.95 each and variegated Euonymus $12.95 each.

Be patient. Do the math. It's worth the wait! This summer I rooted about 400 Burning Bush in just a matter of weeks. It only took a few hours to take the cuttings, prepare them, and stick them in the bed of sand. These plants will be landscape size in three years, four at the most.

Let your imagination run wild. Once you know how to grow your own landscape plants from scratch, just think about all the beautiful and extravagant landscaping ideas you can come up with. Pay close attention to landscaping in your daily travels and while you are on vacation. You'll come up with hundreds of ideas.

The mechanics of starting your own landscape plants from scratch are quite basic for many plants, all you need is a source of cuttings for the plants that you would like to grow yourself, and a little effort. If you see a plant that you would like to try and grow yourself, just ask the owner of the plant if you can take a few clippings. Most people are more than happy to let you have them.

Throughout most of this book I will teach you all about getting your plants started. Before we get to that point, I would like to teach you some basic information about caring for your plants once they are rooted.

Chapter Three

Caring For Your Landscape Plants Once You Have Them Started

Rule number one. Small landscape plants need to be watered on a regular basis. *Too much* water <u>can and will</u> kill just about any landscape plant. This is the most often misunderstood element of landscape gardening. We are all limited by the amount of experience we have in a given field. Through years and years of experience I have gained a great deal of knowledge about landscape plants.

Many people have very limited knowledge of landscape plants because it was probably never and interest of theirs. Then all of a sudden they find themselves in a situation where they need to become landscape gardeners almost overnight. Usually when they just purchased their first home.

They visit the local garden center, buy a few plants, take them home and plant them. Everything goes well and the garden they created looks great. They are extremely proud of what they accomplished. However, in a couple of weeks some of the plants don't look so good. "What could be wrong? I'll bet they need some water." Says the new gardener. "Or maybe they need some fertilizer."

It is possible that water is all they need, but it is highly unlikely that they need fertilizer. If this new gardener has watered these plants at all since they were planted, then water may not be what they need. In so many situations the plants have either been planted too deep, watered too much, or planted in a wet area.

Landscape plants need oxygen just like you and I. They must be planted in soil that is not too heavy, and is well drained. Landscape plants must be able to get oxygen to their root system. If you plant them in soil that does not drain well, the plants are likely to die because the moisture can not escape and the plants suffocate do to a lack of oxygen.

Yet, most novice gardeners do the only thing they know to do. They give the plant more water! Yikes! The plant dies. It's not really the gardeners fault. He or she only did what they thought was right.

Planting a tree or shrub too deep is going to cause the same problem. If you are planting a balled and burlaped plant you should plant it so that about 1-1/2" of the ball is above the ground level. Cover the top of the ball with about 1-1/2" to 2" of soil, creating a mound over the ball. This will allow the transfer of oxygen to the root system, and will actually shed excess water away from the plant.

The same applies to container grown plants. Plant them so that the soil level in the container is slightly above the level of the ground. Make sure you place a layer of soil over top of the soil from the container so the plant does not dry out too easily. There is a very fine line between a plant having enough water, or too much water.

The best way to make sure your plants have the correct amount of moisture in the soil is to raise your planting beds at least 8" with good, rich, well drained topsoil. By planting your trees and shrubs in a raised bed you can water with confidence knowing that excess water will drain away from your landscape plants. Make sure the soil you use to raise your bed does not have a clay base. Clay soil does not drain well at all.

How do you know how wet the soil should be? The easiest way to check the soil for moisture content is to grab a handful of soil from around the root system and squeeze the soil in your hand. If any water at all runs out, the soil is too wet. The soil should be damp and cool to the touch, *but not wet.*

Be careful about following the advice of so called gardening experts. In my opinion, the only person who qualifies as an expert is the person who has planted thousands of landscape plants in every kind of soil imaginable, has guaranteed those plants to live, and has backed up that guarantee with his or her grocery money. That person is an expert!

I say that because I see so many people following the advice of the salesperson in a garden center, or following the planting instructions on a plant tag, and I know what they are doing is likely to kill the plant.

These so called experts recommend that when planting a tree or a shrub you should dig the hole wider and deeper than you need, and filling the bottom with loose stone for drainage, and filling around the sides with a loose organic material. Sounds like a good idea, but if you are in heavy clay soil, you have just created a bathtub for your plant to drown in. You have provided an excellent way for excessive water to get into the hole, but no way for it to drain away. Sure, you put some loose stone in the bottom of the hole for drainage, but what's below the stone? Heavy clay soil, that's what. The water is trapped, and the plant will suffocate.

How to plant depends on the soil you are planting in. If you are planting in sandy soil, or a gravel type soil, then you can dig the hole deeper and wider than you need and use some type of organic material in the bottom and around the sides. If you are in clay you have two choices, either raise the bed 8-10" with good rich topsoil before planting, or plant directly in the clay and back fill around the plant with the clay soil. This will keep excess water from leaching in. In this case, make sure you put the plant in so the root ball is higher than grade. Raising the bed with good rich topsoil is the best solution.

When you start growing your own landscape plants from scratch you are going to root them in a bed or a flat. Once they have established roots you should transplant them to a bed or garden area. The same rules apply. Plant them in a raised bed and don't plant them too deep. Keep them watered, but be careful about over watering.

Fertilizer

There is only one thing you need to know about fertilizer. **"Not enough, is always better than too much."**

Landscape plants are not like the grass around

your home. The grass around your home can grow as much as five inches in one week or more, therefore using up a considerable amount of nitrogen.

Many landscape plants don't grow five inches in a full growing season. You must be extremely careful when applying a fertilizer containing nitrogen to your landscape plants. If you apply more nitrogen than a plant can use, you will burn the plant and likely kill it.

Every fertilizer should have an analysis printed on the container. Such as 12-12-12 , 26-3-3 or 5-10-5. These numbers represent the amount of active chemicals in the fertilizer. The first number represents the nitrogen content, the second number represents the phosphorous content, and the third number represents the potassium content.

A fertilizer with an analysis of 26-3-3 would contain 26% nitrogen, 3% phosphorous, and 3% potassium. The other 68% is just filler material that is neutral. A 26-3-3 fertilizer is very high in nitrogen and should **never** be used on landscape plants. This formula might be all right to use on a lawn during the peak growing season, providing the lawn has an adequate amount of water.

Most nurseries fertilize their landscape plants

with fertilizers that have slow release capabilities. Some of the fertilizers take up to nine months to completely release. This allows the plants to use the fertilizer as it is released.

When fertilizing at home I highly recommend you use organic fertilizers that will not burn. Read the labels carefully. As much as you would like to speed up the growth rate of your landscape plants, fertilizer will help, but it is not a magic wand. The best thing you can do for your landscape plants to keep them healthy, happy, and vigorous, is to plant them in a raised bed of good, rich, well drained topsoil.

Pruning

Proper pruning is an extremely important factor in raising beautiful landscape plants. If you're like most home gardeners, you have a difficult time bringing yourself to prune your plants as they should be pruned. For one, most people don't understand the mechanics of pruning.

Landscape plants primarily have two kinds of buds or branches. Terminal and lateral. The terminal bud is the bud located at the tip of the branch Lateral buds are located along the branch, or on the sides of the branch.

If you are raising evergreen shrubs or deciduous flowering shrubs, it is extremely important that these terminal buds be cut on a regular basis in order for the plant to fill out properly. (A deciduous plant is a plant that is not an evergreen. Deciduous shrubs lose their leaves during the winter months.) A shrub that has been properly pruned will be nice and tight, and full. You can not see through a properly pruned plant. If you do not cut off the terminal bud, the plant just keeps growing in that outward direction with very little development taking place inside the plant.

On the other hand, if you clip that terminal bud, the plant usually sets three or more buds just below where you cut. Allow these buds to develop and grow about four or five inches and cut them again. Just keep doing this until the plant has reached the size you desire. This really does not increase the time it takes to produce a landscape plant. It just assures you of a much nicer plant.

The best time to prune most landscape plants is **when they need it.** It does not harm plants to be pruned during the growing season. If you wait until fall to do your pruning, the plant will have grown considerably and most of that growth will have to been pruned away.

Diagram 1. The shrub on the left represents a plant that has not been pruned. Notice how it is growing tall but very thin inside. By pruning this plant as in the middle drawing, and continuing to clip the terminal buds, you can develop a very nice, tight, and compact shrub like the drawing on the right.

      On the other hand, if you clip that terminal bud during the growing season, the plant will set three more buds within a matter of weeks. These buds will begin to grow and the plant can be pruned again before the end of the growing season.

      Take a look at diagram 1. on page 21. As you can see, if you plant a shrub in the spring with three terminal branches and don't prune it at all, at the end of the growing season you will have a very tall shrub with only three branches, but if you prune that shrub at the time of planting, and at least once more during the growing season, you will end up with a smaller shrub, but much nicer. That smaller shrub will develop into a beautiful plant and be an asset to your landscape for many years to come.

If you're raising a tree the rules are different. With trees you want to leave the terminal bud intact until the tree has reached the height where you would like the branches to start. So basically, just let the tree grow straight up like a whip until it reaches a height of about five feet.

At that point, cut the top of the tree off below the terminal bud at the height where you would like the branches to start. Then as the head of the tree begins to develop, prune it much the same as you would for the shrubs we discussed earlier.

This young tree is going to have leaves and small branches developing along the lower portion of the stem. It's all right to leave these on the stem until the tree has developed a small head. The plant needs these leaves for food development.

Once the tree has established a small head go ahead and remove any leaves or branches along the stem of the tree. Keep pruning the terminal buds on the branches of the tree, in order to form a tree with a tight, compact head.

The final word on pruning is this: **Just do**

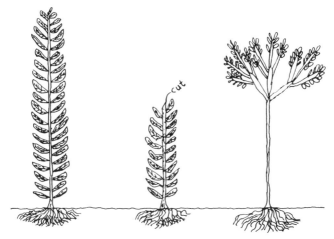

Diagram 2. The drawing on the left shows a small tree, most likely grown from seed, growing straight up. Clip the top of the tree off at the height you want the branches to start. The tree will begin to develop a head at that point. Once the tree has developed a small head, the leaves and small branches along the lower portion of the stem can be removed.

it!!! Don't be afraid to trim those plants. It will not hurt them.

The best time to trim Rhododendrons and Azaleas is right after they bloom because they quickly start setting flower buds for next year. If you wait until fall or spring, then you will cut off some of the flower buds. This will not harm the plant, it just won't be as pretty when it flowers, but if you forget to prune right after they bloom, don't wait until next year, go ahead and trim even if it does cost you a few blooms.

The ideal time to trim most other plants is late fall or early spring, but <u>anytime</u> is better than not at all.

Now that you have all of this basic information firmly locked into your brain, let's get on to growing some landscape plants from scratch.

The next section of this book will describe the many different propagation techniques for landscape plants. Don't get nervous. It's a breeze!

Keep in mind that in this section I do not give you specific information for all of the plants that can be propagated using these different techniques. Specific information for each type of plant can be found in the back of this book in the **"How to do What"** section.

Chapter Four

Division

Division is a propagation technique used for landscape plants that do not have a single stem or crown. Many plants have just one stem emerging from the ground and can not be propagated using this technique. However, there are quite a few different plants that have multiple stems emerging from the ground and can be propagated through division.

A few examples would be Hostas, Mums, Ornamental Grasses, and many perennial flowers.

Division is exactly as it sounds. You just dig up the parent plant that you intend to reproduce and quite simply divide it into many plants. Of course the size of the parent plant will determine how many times you can divide it.

If you don't care to reduce the size of the parent plant, then you would only remove a few divisions from around the edge of the parent plant. You can probably do so without actually removing the parent plant from the ground. Just scrape the ground clean around the plant so you can see exactly which sections of the parent plant you would like to remove, take a spade and force it into the ground between the parent plant and the division you are removing. Make three more cuts around the piece you are removing, completely severing the division from the parent plant, and cutting all the roots securing it in the ground. Pry the division out of the ground. Trim the roots a little if needed and replant the division in it's new location.

However, if you don't mind reducing the size of the parent plant you can completely divide the parent plant into small, equal size pieces.

Early spring is a good time to propagate by division, however, late fall will work as well. Propagation by division should be done when the parent plant is either dormant, or about to break dormancy in the spring.

The dormancy season begins in the fall after the first good hard freeze, not necessarily a frost, A frost is usually not severe enough to trigger dormancy. It usually takes a good hard freeze when the temperature drops down below 32 degrees F. for a period of a few hours. It's pretty easy to determine when a good hard freeze has taken place because any leaves remaining on the trees will be crinkled and severely damaged. Many will fall to the ground the next day.

And of course once dormancy begins the plants remain dormant until spring arrives and the temperatures begin to increase. As the temperature increases the plants become active. Root activity can occur throughout the winter, anytime the soil temperature rise above 45 degrees F. The plants are not officially out of dormancy until leaves begin to appear.

Most people don't realize that nurserymen can only dig deciduous plants while they are dormant. Once a deciduous plant develops leaves in the spring, it can not safely be transplanted until late fall when it is dormant again. Digging a deciduous plant once it leafs out will immediately put the plant into shock, and likely kill it.

Evergreens are a little different. They can not be safely transplanted once new growth is established in the spring, but once that new growth hardens off later in the summer, evergreens can be transplanted. Of course, transplanting during dormancy is usually the safest bet.

Back to propagating by division. To divide a plant all you do is dig up the parent plant. The entire plant will come out of the ground in one large clump. Place this clump on a hard surface and just cut it into several pieces using a large knife or even a spade. Each division should have at least two or three sprouts or eyes. This is much easier to determine in early spring once the eyes have begun to develop, but the leaves have not yet developed.

Once you have made these divisions, just replant each division back into your garden. Keep them watered, but not soaked.

Division is a very simple form of propagation, but it is only effective with a limited number of plants. Division will not work on what would be considered the higher forms of landscape plants. If a plant has a single stem emerging from the ground, then it must be propagated by another means.

Chapter Five

Layering

Layering is another simple form of propagation that can be done at home without special equipment. Layering is a natural form of propagation that often takes place inadvertently. Layering usually is most effective with deciduous shrubs. However, I have seen broad leaf evergreens such as Rhododendrons, and Piers Japonica propagate themselves through inadvertent layering.

Inadvertent layering is something that happens both in the natural environment of a woods, or in a commercial nursery. In the woods, the lower branches of a plant get pulled to the ground from their own weight, or because of snow sticking to or laying on the branches. As the branches lay on the ground, all of the necessary conditions exist for the plant to develop roots at the point that the branch is resting on the ground.

In a commercial nursery many shrubs are planted in rows. The rows are cultivated on a regular basis to keep weed growth to a minimum. Through the cultivation process a few branches can be inadvertently, but partially covered with soil. When

Diagram 3. Propagation through layering is as simple as pulling a branch down to the ground and covering it with soil. Wounding the stem at the point shown in this drawing will help to stimulate root development. A wire loop can be placed over the layered branch to hold it down.

this happens the plants often develop roots at the point that they were covered with soil.

To layer a plant all you do is dig a small hole near the base of the shrub, pull down one of the lower branches, bending it in a U, and force the bottom of the U in the hole leaving the end of the branch stick up out of the ground. The portion of the stem that is covered with soil will develop roots. See Diagram 3.

Making a small wound on the portion of the stem that is to be buried will help to stimulate root development. To make this wound, using a knife, simply make an angled cut into the stem. Make the cut about 1/2" long, cutting into the stem not quite half way. As you bend the stem to force it into the hole, be careful not to break the stem at the cut. You can also wound the stem by simply scraping off about 1/2" of bark with a knife.

It is also beneficial to treat the wounded area with a powder root inducing compound available at most garden centers.

Some branches are more rigid than others. It may be necessary to anchor the branch down using a piece of heavy wire bent in a U, or a fork shaped branch. Or you can hold the branch down by placing some form of weight on the soil covering the branch.

Layering can be done in the fall or spring. You should achieve great success with layering as late as the middle of May. Layering yields great success on many deciduous shrubs because you are not actually removing the branch from the plant at the time of the layering process. The new plant that you are attempting to propagate is still attached to, and being nurtured by the parent plant throughout the entire process.

Even though layering can be done until mid May, I would suggest that you do your layering as early as possible in the spring to give the plant ample time to establish an extensive root system.

If you layer a plant in the fall, you should not attempt to remove that layer from the parent plant until the following fall or spring. Do not disturb the layer while the plant is actively growing, wait until the plant is dormant.

If you layer a plant in the spring, you might be able to remove it from the parent in the fall after the growing season has ended, but I would leave it alone until spring. If you have a mild winter and the soil temperatures are fairly warm, further root development might take place over the winter months.

Liners planted out in the fall can often be forced out of the ground by the freezing and thawing process. (Small plants are often called "liners", short for lining out stock.) That's why I prefer to do most of my planting of small plants in the spring.

Since the invention of intermittent misting equipment, not very many commercial nurseries use layering as a means of propagation. It is too labor intensive for the number of new layers a nursery can obtain. It also ties up valuable field space that could be used for more productive things. Keep in mind that wholesale nurseries produce plants by the tens of thousands. Nurseries have to keep a whole block of 'stock' plants that are to be used for nothing but layering. A good stock plant might yield 30 or 40 layers, where the same 'stock' plant could yield several hundred softwood cuttings. Understanding how the commercial nurserymen do layering will help you achieve better results at home.

Most deciduous shrubs have the ability to put on 18-36" of new growth each year. This new growth is the ideal wood for layering. If you prune the shrub heavily the year before you intend to use it for layering, it will produce a substantial amount of new growth that will be ideal for the layering process. I would actually cut the shrub to within six or seven inches from the ground. This would force the shrub to put out many new branches the following growing season. In the fall of the same season, this new growth would still be fairly pliable and could be easily pulled to the ground to be layered.

Once these new layers are rooted they can be removed by cutting the branch just below where the new roots have developed. At the same time, the parent plant should be cut back just like before, and it will produce more new growth for the next layering season.

Serpentine Layering

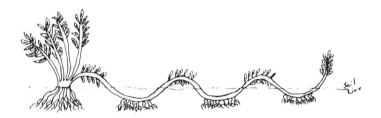

Diagram 4. Serpentine layering is a technique you can use to get a few more offspring from each parent plant.

You can also do what is known as Serpentine Layering. Serpentine layering is done exactly the same way as regular layering, with the exception that if the branch you are layering is long enough, you can loop it underground more than once. See diagram 4.

In order to do serpentine layering, you must leave a few buds exposed to the air and sunlight after each loop that dips underground. Each one of these loops will develop into a new plant.

Air Layering

Air layering is a propagation technique using

Photograph 1. Air layering is a propagation technique you can use on plants where you can not pull a branch down to the ground. With this technique you actually pack damp peat moss around the branch and wrap it with plastic.

the same theory as regular layering, except you don't bury the branch in the ground. Instead you can use a branch up much higher on the plant, wound the stem as with regular layering, apply a powder rooting compound to the wounded area, pack damp peat moss around that branch, and wrap it in plastic. See photograph 1.

This type of layering can be effective, but it is more time consuming. When you wrap this layered area with plastic film, you must make the seal on each end tight enough as to not allow the moisture to escape. By the same token, you must be careful not to girdle the plant by making these ties too tight.

You must keep an eye on your air layers for the duration of the time it will take to develop roots. If there does not appear to be any beads of moisture on the inside of the plastic film, you should add water to the peat moss. You should be able to do this without unwrapping the film by using a plastic cooking syringe. Just poke a hole in the plastic, add some water, and put tape over the hole when you are done.

Air layering should be done in the early spring, so root development can be complete by fall. It is best to remove air layers from the parent plant before winter.

Unlike regular layers that are protected from the extreme cold by the insulation provided by snow cover, air layers would be exposed to temperatures far too extreme, if left attached to the parent plant through the winter months.

Chapter Six

Softwood Cuttings of Deciduous Plants

What is a softwood cutting? To help you understand softwood cuttings and hardwood cuttings let's use a Burning Bush as an example.

If you watch closely as a Burning Bush develop buds in the early spring, you will see how these little tiny buds quickly develop into new growth shoots, 6" to 8" in length. These new shoots develop very quickly, once the plant begins to grow in the spring. This new growth is very soft and pliable.

As the growing season progresses, this new growth becomes harder and more rigid. By fall this new growth has hardened off to the point that it is almost brittle.

The only difference between a softwood cutting and a hardwood cutting is the time of year you take the cutting. Both are of the current seasons growth. It is always recommended that the cuttings you use are of the current years growth. If you go too deep into a plant to take your cuttings, you are likely to get into wood that is more than one year old.

Using this older wood is almost certain to hamper your results.

Propagation of softwood cuttings is usually done at the end of May or the beginning of June depending on the climate you are in. Trying to do softwood cuttings prior to that is a waste of time because the wood is too soft and will wilt down very quickly. The ideal time to take softwood cuttings is just as the wood begins to harden off.

Here in northeastern Ohio, June 1st is usually our target date. Plants in this area are usually a little behind the plants in southern Ohio. We are sitting right on the southern shore of Lake Erie. When that huge body of water freezes over for the winter, it is slow to thaw and warm up. Therefore, the temperature here stays a little cooler in the spring. Of course it works just the opposite in the fall and the lake is usually responsible for sparing us from the first few frosts.

Softwood cuttings of many deciduous plants root very quickly and easily under the right conditions. However, controlling the conditions is critical. Softwood cuttings are very delicate and can dehydrate very easily, especially under the summer sun. However, with the warm temperatures of June, and the tenderness of softwood cuttings, root

Diagram 5. This drawing represents a softwood cutting and how it should be stripped and wounded to help induce root development.

development will occur very quickly, if you can keep the cuttings from dehydrating.

The absolute best way to root softwood cuttings is by sticking them in a bed of very course sand and watering them very lightly for just a few seconds, every five or ten minutes, for a period of two to six weeks. Of course this is impossible, unless you have an automatic watering system known as an intermittent mist system.

I will go into much greater detail about intermittent mist in a later chapter of this book. I am bringing it up here so you will know exactly what intermittent mist does, and how it works. Knowing what it does gives you an idea of what conditions you must try and create in order to achieve success with softwood cuttings at home, without expensive equipment.

Preparing a softwood cutting is easy. Just clip a cutting about 4" in length from the parent plant. Take only tip cuttings. In other words, just take one cutting from each branch, the top four inches of each branch. This is the newest growth. Strip the leaves off the lower two thirds of the cutting, leaving just a stem and a few leaves at the top.

Wounding the cutting slightly can help the rooting process. You can wound the cutting by scraping the side of the stem lightly from the bottom of the cutting up 1/2". See diagram 5.

It is always beneficial to treat your cuttings with a liquid or a powder rooting compound just prior to sticking them. Rooting compounds are available at most garden centers and do help to stimulate root development. It really doesn't matter whether you use a liquid or a powder. There are different strengths available in the powder formulas. Hardwood cuttings require a stronger formula than softwood cuttings.

Most liquid rooting compounds are sold in

concentrate form and must be diluted with water. I like the liquid because all you have to do is adjust the amount of water you add depending on whether you are doing softwood or hardwood cuttings. There are instructions on the package.

The best growing medium for softwood cuttings is a **very course** grade of sand. You do not want to stick the cuttings in soil. The sand you use must be course. When you water the sand, the water should run right through. The sand should have very little moisture retention ability. The stems of softwood cuttings rot very easily.

Preparing an area to stick your cuttings is quite simple. For softwood cuttings all you need is a wooden or plastic flat, or a small raised bed. I recommend using flats for softwood cuttings, so you can start them in the shade and move them into the sun after a period of 7-10 days.

The flats should be 3-4" deep. Fill them to the top with course sand. Make your cuttings as described earlier, dip them in a rooting compound, and stick them in the flat. It helps to make a hole or a slice in the sand first, so the cutting will slide in easier. Softwood cuttings are not very rigid. They will break if you try and force them into the sand. Using a putty knife or a masonry trowel you can slice an opening through the sand, or use a large screw driver to make a hole in the sand. Space your cuttings about 1" apart in the flat. Firm the sand around the cuttings as you stick them, you do not want air pockets around the stems. You can also water thoroughly the first time to make sure all of the voids are filled.

It is said that the ideal time to take softwood cuttings is early in the morning. However, that is not always convenient for me, so I have taken them at all hours of the day. I have never been able to determine whether or not morning, noon, or night yielded the best results.

Softwood cuttings wilt very quickly. Take just a few cuttings at a time and get them stuck in the sand and watered as quickly as possible. When you first take the cuttings, keep them in the shade for a period of 7-10 days. This gives them a chance to harden off before you put them in the sun. Plants need at least partial sun in order to develop roots.

Water them lightly, as often as you can, especially the first few days. Proper watering is critical. The ideal situation is to apply a very light spray of water for just a few seconds, allow that water to evaporate off almost completely, and then water again. Of course this is next to impossible without automatic equipment, but if you can at least water lightly every couple of hours the first day or so, you should realize some degree of success.

If your first batch of softwood cuttings do poorly, try a new batch as soon as you realize your first batch is failing. Just a few days can make a remarkable difference in the texture of the wood as the new growth matures. Cuttings that wilt down almost immediately one day might do 100% better two days later. As the new growth matures, the wood hardens off, and the cuttings become more durable. Of course the harder wood takes a little longer to establish roots.

Softwood cuttings are delicate and somewhat difficult, but if you can keep them from wilting they will root very quickly. Hardwood cuttings are much easier, but it takes considerably longer to establish roots on hardwood cuttings. Also, there are some plants that are difficult to root using the hardwood method.

If you are an avid gardener, you might consider setting up an intermittent mist system in your backyard. The amount of space required is very small, but there is an investment in the equipment. Maybe a friend or neighbor is also an avid gardener and would like to go together with you to share the cost of an intermittent mist system. Ordering and cost information can be found in the back of this book, after the index.

Intermittent mist makes rooting softwood cuttings like child's play. As a matter of fact, when my youngest son was in the first grade, he took softwood cuttings, stripped the cuttings, dipped them in the rooting compound, and stuck them in the sand. That's all there is to it, the intermittent mist system does the rest. You'll learn more about intermittent mist later in this book.

If you happen to be the owner or manager of a business, you might consider setting up an intermittent mist system at your place of business for all the employees to use. Each employee could have their own flat. If you put the cuttings in fairly tight, you can get over 100 cuttings in a flat. I am not a tax accountant, but I would think there could be a tax savings here, not to mention what it would do for employee moral. The employees families could get involved. It's something to think about.

Chapter Seven

Softwood Cuttings of Evergreens

Doing softwood cuttings of evergreens is just about the same as with deciduous plants. Except with evergreens you should wait until later in the summer before taking the cuttings. You can start taking your evergreen cuttings around the Fourth of July and continue taking cuttings through August.

Some of the evergreens that can be done as softwood cuttings are Taxus, Junipers, Arborvitae, Dwarf Alberta Spruce, Rhododendrons, Azaleas, Japanese Holly and Euonymus.

Evergreen cuttings should be stuck in flats filled with coarse sand, or in a raised bed of coarse sand. Wounding the cuttings isn't necessary because stripping the needles off causes enough minor injury to induce the development of callous.

Waiting until later in the fall, and doing evergreens as hardwood cuttings requires less effort, but you lose the benefit of the warm temperatures available to you in July and August. Cuttings root much quicker if the sun can warm the growing medium to a temperature of 70 degrees F.

If you wait until the end of August, you can still benefit from the warm temperatures to initiate the rooting process, and within a few weeks the temperatures will drop, reducing the amount of care required.

The rules for watering softwood evergreen cuttings are about the same as for deciduous plants. Evergreens don't require quite as much water, but they still need care on a regular basis.

As with deciduous plants, intermittent mist works really great for softwood evergreens as well.

Chapter Eight

Hardwood Cuttings of Deciduous Plants

There are two different ways to do hardwood cuttings of deciduous plants. Is one better than the other? I really don't know. It depends on exactly what you are rooting, what the soil conditions are at your house, and what Mother Nature has up her sleeve for the coming winter. I have experienced both success and failure using each method. Only experimentation will determine what works best for you. Try some cuttings using each method.

When doing hardwood cuttings of deciduous plants, you should wait until the parent plants are completely dormant. As mentioned earlier, this does not happen until you have had a good hard freeze where the temperature dips down below 32 degrees F. for a period of several hours. Here in northeastern Ohio this usually occurs around mid November.

Method Number One

As you recall when we discussed softwood cuttings of deciduous plants, I told you to take tip cuttings from the ends of the branches only. That rule does not apply to hardwood cuttings of deciduous plants.

For instance, a plant such as Forsythia can grow as much as four feet in one season. In that case, you can use all of the current years growth to make hardwood cuttings. You might be able to get six or eight cuttings from one branch.

Grapes are extremely vigorous. A grape vine can grow up to ten feet or more in one season. That entire vine can be used for hardwood cuttings. Of course with grape vines, there is considerable space between the buds, so the cuttings have to be much longer than most other deciduous plants. The average length of a hardwood grape vine cutting is about 12" and still only has 3 or 4 buds.

The bud spacing on most other deciduous plants is much closer, so the cuttings only need to be about 6-8" in length.

Since hardwood cuttings must be done during the winter months, you probably will want to work in your garage or basement where it is not quite so cold. Of course there are still some nice days after the first freeze when working outside is possible.

Making a deciduous hardwood cutting is

quite easy. Just collect some branches (known as canes) from the parent plants. Clip these canes into cuttings about 6" long. Of course these canes will not have any leaves on them because the plant is dormant, but if you examine the canes closely you will see little bumps along the cane. These bumps are bud unions. They are next years leaf buds or nodes, as they are often called. When making a hardwood cutting of a deciduous plant, it is best to make the cut at the bottom, or the butt end of the cutting just below a node, and make the cut at the top of the cutting about 3/4" above a node.

This technique serves two purposes. One, it makes it easier for you to distinguish the top of the cutting from the bottom of the cutting as you handle them. It also aids the cutting in two different ways.

Any time you cut a plant above a node, the section of stem left above that node will die back to the top node. So if you were to leave 1/2" of stem below the bottom node, it would just die back anyway. Having that section of dead wood underground is not a good idea. It is only a place for insects and disease to hide.

It is also helpful to actually injure a plant slightly when trying to force it to develop roots. When a plant is injured, it develops a callous over the

Diagram 6. This drawing represents a hardwood cutting of a deciduous plant. The dark spots along the cutting are the nodes, or bud unions. Notice how the cut at the bottom of the cutting is just below a node, and is a straight cut. The cut at the top of the cutting is 3/4" above a node and is an angle cut. The section of stem above the top node (indicated with an X) will die. The purpose of leaving this section of the cutting is to protect the buds of the top node as you handle and plant the cutting. You can use this section as a handle to push the cutting into the ground as you plant it.

wound as protection. This callous build up is necessary before roots will develop. Cutting just below a node on the bottom of a cutting causes the plant to develop callous and eventually, roots.

Making the cut on the top of the cutting 3/4" above the node is done so that the 3/4" section of stem above the node will provide protection for the top node. This keeps the buds from being damaged or knocked off during handling and planting. You can press down on the cutting without harming the buds. Although not necessary, it helps to make the cut at the top of the cutting at an angle. This sheds water away from the cut end of the cutting and helps to keep disease and insects away from the cuttings.

Once you have all of your cuttings made, dip them in a rooting compound. Make sure you have the right strength rooting compound for hardwood cuttings.

Line them up so the butt ends are even and tie them into bundles. Select a spot in your garden that is in full sun. Dig a hole about 10" deep and large enough to hold all of the bundles of cuttings. Place the bundles of cuttings in the hole **upside down.** The butt ends of the cuttings should be up. The butt ends of the cuttings should be about 3" below the surface. Cover the cuttings completely with soil and mark the location with a stake, so you can find them again in the spring.

Over the winter the cuttings will develop callous and possibly some roots. Placing them in the hole upside down puts the butt ends closest to the surface, so they can be warmed by the sun, creating favorable conditions for root development. Being upside down also discourages top growth.

Leave them alone until about mid spring after the danger of frost has passed. Over the winter the buds will begin to develop and will be quite tender when you dig them up. Frost could do considerable damage if you dig them and plant them out too early.

That's why it is best to leave them buried until the danger of frost has passed.

Dig them up very carefully, so as not to damage them. Cut open the bundles and examine the butt ends. Hopefully, you will see some callous build up. Even if there is no callous, plant them out anyway.

You don't need a bed of sand or anything special when you plant the cuttings out. Just put them in a sunny location in your garden. Of course the area you chose should be well drained, with good rich topsoil.

To plant the cuttings, just dig a very narrow trench, or using a spade, make a slice by prying open the ground. Place the cuttings in the trench with the butt ends down. Bury about one half of the cutting leaving a few buds above ground. Back fill around the cuttings with loose soil making sure there are no air pockets. Tamp them in lightly. Water them on a regular basis, but don't make the soil so wet that they rot.

Within a few weeks the cuttings will start to leaf out. Some will more than likely collapse because there are not enough roots to support the plant. The others will develop roots as they leaf out. By fall, the cuttings that survived should be pretty well rooted. You can transplant them once they are dormant, or you can wait until spring. If you wait until spring, make sure you transplant them before they break dormancy.

There are many wholesale nurseries where the employees spend a great deal of their time during the winter months making hardwood cuttings using this method. Years ago I worked for a nursery that produced hundreds of thousands of grape plants each year. The owner of the nursery expected us to produce 5,000 cuttings each day. Of course he would give us about two weeks to work our way up to that figure. Once we were able to make 5,000 a day, he would then put us on piece work. We earned eight hours wages for 5,000 cuttings. Eventually I was able to make 5,000 cuttings in six hours.

Method Number Two

When using the second method for rooting hardwood cuttings of deciduous plants you do everything exactly the same as you do with method number one, up to the point where you bury them for the winter.

With method number two you don't bury them at all. Instead, you plant the cuttings out as soon as you make them in the late fall. In other words, you just completely skip the step where you bury the cuttings underground for the winter.

Plant them exactly the same way as described for method number one. As with all cuttings, treating them with a rooting compound prior to planting will help induce root growth.

You can do hardwood cuttings of deciduous plants throughout most of the winter, as long as the ground is not frozen.

Hardwood cuttings work fairly well for most of the deciduous shrubs. However, they are not likely to work for some of the more refined varieties of deciduous ornamentals. If your curious about how to propagate a particular plant, just check the **"How to Do What"** section in the back of this book.

Chapter Nine

Hardwood Cuttings of Evergreens

Hardwood cuttings of evergreens are usually done after you have experienced two heavy frosts in the late fall, around mid November or so. But I have obtained good results with some plants doing them as early as mid September, taking advantage of the warmth of the fall sun. Try some cuttings early and if they do poorly, just do some more in November.

Hardwood cuttings of many evergreens can be done at home in a simple frame filled with course sand. To make such a frame, just make a square or rectangular frame using 2" by 6" boards. Nail the four corners together as if to make a large picture frame. This frame should sit on top of the ground in an area that is well drained. An area of partial shade is preferred.

Once you have the frame constructed remove any weeds or grass inside the frame so this vegetation does not grow up through your propagation bed. Fill this frame with a **very course** grade of sand. This frame must be well drained. Standing water is sure to seriously hamper your results.

Making the evergreen cuttings is easy. Just clip a cutting 4-5 inches in length from the parent plant. Make tip cuttings only. Strip the needles or leaves from the bottom one half to two thirds of the cutting. Wounding evergreen cuttings isn't usually necessary because removing the leaves or needles causes enough injury for callous build up and root development.

Dip the butt ends of the cuttings in a powder or liquid rooting compound and stick them in the sand about 3/4" to 1" apart. Keep them watered throughout the fall until cool temperatures set in. Start watering again in the spring and throughout the summer. They don't need a lot of water, but be careful not to let them dry out. And at the same time making sure they are not soaking wet.

Hardwood cuttings of many evergreens will root this way, but it does take some time. You should leave them in the frame for a period of twelve months. You can leave them longer if you like. Leaving them until the following spring would be just fine. They should develop more roots over the winter.

A friend of mine who is a wholesale nurseryman uses this method to root all most all of his evergreens. He covers his frames with steel hoops and plastic to provide some extra protection over the winter. This can help, but you must be careful. Do not use clear plastic. It will get too hot on the nice days and the plants will start to come out of dormancy too early. Then they will freeze back when the temperature dips back down below freezing. If you are going to cover your frame for the winter use white plastic or clear plastic that has been white washed with white latex paint. You must also water during the winter if you are going to cover the plants with plastic. Dehydration occurs very easily during the winter.

For the home gardener I recommend not covering the frame for the winter. A covering of light fluffy snow actually protects plants from harsh winter winds. Let Mother Nature take care of your cuttings over the winter. Sometimes she does a fantastic job, and sometimes she reminds us that we are tinkering with nature.

This method of rooting hardwood cuttings can and will work for a variety of different evergreen plants, both needled and broadleaf evergreens. But there are some varieties that are more difficult and will not root unless special care is provided. For most of the more difficult to root evergreens, the addition of bottom heat will help to induce root development. We will discuss bottom heat in the next section of this book.

Keep in mind that any time we attempt to root a cutting of any kind, we are asking the plant to establish roots before the top of the plant starts growing. Once the plant begins to grow it will die if it has not established roots first. Softwood cuttings are very delicate and will collapse if not cared for carefully. However, softwood cuttings root very quickly and can be growing on their own roots in a matter of a few weeks. Hardwood cuttings on the other hand are much more durable and can survive for months with very little care or roots. However, hardwood cuttings are very slow to develop roots.

It's a matter of what works best for you.

Chapter Ten

Bottom Heat

Landscape plants love heat. When they are warm they grow. When they are cool they do not grow. Of course as with everything else, extreme heat is not good.

We know that root growth can and will begin taking place once soil temperatures reach or exceed 45 degrees F. Even if the top of a plant is not active, the roots can be actively growing underground, if the soil is adequately warm.

Professional growers have learned that if you can heat the soil or other growing medium without raising the air temperature around the tops of the plants, root development can be induced and or speeded.

This technique is used by professional propagators around the world. The same evergreens that require up to twelve months to develop roots, as discussed in the previous section, can be successfully rooted in as little as six weeks by applying bottom heat.

The secret to using this technique is to warm the soil without increasing the air temperature above the soil. In a commercial nursery the ideal situation is to maintain a soil temperature of 69-70 degrees F. and an air temperature of 40-45 degrees F.

Nurserymen use different ways to accomplish this. One of the most popular ways is to set the propagation frames on benches about 36" high inside a greenhouse. Using a small forced air furnace they blow the warm air under the benches. The benches have plastic or some other material around the bottom so the heat can not escape out the sides. The heat must rise up through the growing medium. A special thermostat is inserted in the soil. This thermostat controls the furnace. When the soil reaches the optimum temperature the heat is turned off until it is needed again.

Trapping the heat under the bench keeps the air temperature much lower than the soil temperature. Therefore, rooting activity can take place while the top of the cuttings remain dormant.

Professional growers also use very complex systems that circulate hot water through plastic lines buried in the soil. This works well, but a second heating system is usually required to keep the air around the top of the cuttings from getting too cold.

Nurserymen are innovative people. Some of them have used regular household water heaters, installed a circulating pump, and circulated hot water through 1" plastic piping. When you consider a hot water boiler sells for $900. or more, this is a great idea. A new household water heater can be purchased for around $150.

For you and I at home these systems are too complex. After all, we're only interested in rooting a few cuttings or maybe a few hundred,   not fifty or sixty thousand. So how can we use bottom heat to increase our results and to cut down on the amount of time it takes to root our cuttings.

Although I have never used the method I am about to describe, I have friend in the nursery business who uses it. When they build their frame for their hardwood cuttings they dig a hole the size of the frame, about two feet deep, exactly where they are going to set the frame. They pack this hole full of manure all the way up to ground level. They then set the frame over this bed of manure and fill the frame with course sand just as described earlier.

Through the natural process of decomposition the manure heats up as it decomposes. This heat warms the sand in the propagating frame. Now I doubt that you will ever achieve a soil temperature of 69 degrees F., but at 45 degrees F. rooting can begin.

An easier way to create bottom heat in your propagating frame would be to purchase an electric soil warming cable kit. These soil warming cables are available from garden centers or mail order garden supply companies.

To install them just bury them as you fill your frame with sand. Put an inch or two of sand in your frame depending on how deep your frame is, and then lay the electric cables in the sand and place the rest of the sand on top of the cables. The cables should be about 3-4 inches down in the sand.

Make sure you buy a soil warming kit with a built in thermostat. These thermostats are preset and can not be changed. The ideal soil temperature for rooting most cuttings is 69 degrees F.

Make sure the electric cables do not touch each other when you install them. They are insulated, but two cables touching one another could cause a short circuit. The best way to accomplish this is to buy a piece of hardware cloth (screen) the size of your propagating frame. This hardware cloth should have large holes, at least 1/4" or more. Lay the soil warming cables on the screen and tie them in place using string or twist ties. **Do not make these ties tight.** Be careful not to cut into the insulation on the wires.

Once this is done, just lay the hardware cloth in the bottom of your propagating frame. Be careful when sticking cuttings or removing cuttings not to damage the soil warming cables.

The thermostat is built right into the soil warming cables. It should be buried in the sand. Make sure the thermostat is not right up against a cable. Placing the thermostat too close to a cable will give it a false reading and the proper soil temperature will not be maintained.

The soil warming cable kit that you purchase will come with instructions. Read them carefully.

Bottom heat can also be used to induce and speed the rooting of hardwood cuttings of deciduous plants. Purple Sandcherry is an extremely popular landscape plant. This plant does not do well from softwood cuttings, unless you have an intermittent mist system. They can be grown from hardwood cuttings, but the percentage that actually root, is usually not high. However, if you make your cuttings as described in chapter 8, tie them in bundles, and place them right side up in a bed of coarse sand equipped with bottom heat for a period of 14-20 days, the cuttings will develop callous and be ready to plant out with a much higher degree of success.

Some plants are extremely difficult to root using other methods. Rhododendrons for instance are very slow if they root at all using other methods, but with bottom heat they root quite fast.

Hey! How about me and you staying in touch?

You can keep in touch with the author of this book and learn a variety of landscape gardening techniques, including landscape design ideas, by subscribing to my quarterly newsletter. There is much more that I could not cover in this book. Look in the back of this book for information about my newsletter, videos, and other landscape gardening offers.

Chapter Eleven

Intermittent Mist

Intermittent mist is used primarily for softwood and semi-softwood cuttings of both deciduous plants and evergreens.

As you learned earlier in the section regarding softwood cuttings, they will root very quickly under the right conditions, but softwood cuttings are extremely delicate and will expire quickly, if not properly tended to.

Intermittent mist is like hiring a full time nanny for your softwood cuttings. An intermittent mist system automatically applies a very small amount of water every few minutes, all day long, until your cuttings are rooted.

Even though intermittent mist is off and on through out the day, the actual amount of water used is quite low. The water nozzles are very small, allowing only a minimum amount of water to pass through. When the water is on, the duration of spray is only about seven seconds.

Once the sun goes down the mist system can

Photograph 2. This is a Burning Bush rooted cutting. Under intermittent mist Burning Bush root quite easily in just a matter of three of four weeks.

be turned off until the next morning. I actually have two timers on my mist system. One to control the cycle during the daylight hours, and the second timer is a 24 hour timer I use to turn the system off and on each morning and evening, automatically.

For instance, a typical intermittent mist system with freshly stuck softwood cuttings would have a cycle as follows; water on every five minutes for a duration of seven seconds. If you started this cycle at 8:00 a.m. and allowed it to run automatically until 8:00 p.m., the actual "on" time would be less than seventeen minutes for the entire day.

The intermittent mist system you use should

Photograph 3. It's difficult to see in this photo, but in my right hand I am holding a Burning Bush rooted cutting. To my left is a Burning Bush that we grew in the field in just four years from a rooted cutting just like the one I am holding.

be completely adjustable. You should be able to adjust how often your cuttings are watered, and the duration, or the length of time the spray of water stays on. The nozzles used for the actual spray should be quite fine. The secret is to apply a very fine spray of water on a frequent basis.

When you first take your softwood cuttings and stick them in the bed of course sand, it is a good idea to water them quite frequently for the first few days until they harden off. After four or five days you can water them less often, but still quite frequently.

When I first start sticking my softwood

Photograph 4. This is one of the mini spray nozzles used with an intermittent mist system. This nozzle sprays a pattern approximately 5' in diameter. The water droplets are very small, delivering only a small amount of water.

cuttings around the first week of June the cuttings are very soft and delicate, so delicate that I only make a small amount of cuttings and immediately get them under the mist.

I set my system to water the cuttings every five minutes for a period of seven seconds. After a period of four or five days I change the settings. I then go to ten minute intervals and stay with a seven second spray of water.

Intermittent mist sounds much more complicated than it really is. However, it does require an investment in equipment and the proper controls. Once you own the equipment you can

Photograph 5. The two wooden frames in the foreground of this photo contain about 5,000 cutting that we are rooting using intermittent mist. As you can see in this small area we can start thousands of cuttings. Each of these frames are 4 feet by 7 feet.

produce hundreds, if not thousands of **"Free"** landscape plants each year. Intermittent mist is fun because the cuttings root so quickly. Some plants will start showing roots in about two weeks.

An intermittent mist system requires only four major components. The small spray nozzles that deliver a very fine mist of water, a 24 volt transformer, a 24 volt electric solenoid valve to control the flow of water, and a timer with the ability to control the solenoid valve with intervals as close as every three minutes. For safety reasons I highly recommend that you use 24 volt controls.

I have a complete and ready to use intermittent mist system that I offer for sale to

anybody who is interested. There is information on
how to order this system in the back of the book.
This is the very same equipment I use.

I love propagating with intermittent mist. It
amazes me. It is so easy, it is almost like magic. You
stick the cuttings in the sand, turn on the mist system
and walk away. Some plants root so quickly under
intermittent mist that when you come back to check
on them in a couple of weeks you can't even pull a
cutting out of the sand because it has developed so
many roots that it is firmly anchored in the bed of
sand.

All you have to worry about is a power
failure. If for some reason the electricity supply to
your home is temporarily interrupted, you should
keep the cuttings watered by hand until the power is
restored. Of course this is only a problem during the
daylight hours. If it happens to be an overcast day
and there is no direct sunlight on the cuttings they
won't need much water. On the other hand if it is a
hot sunny day, watering is extremely important.

If I experience a power failure on a hot, sunny
day I hook my mist system directly to a garden hose,
by-passing the electric solenoid valve, and allow the
water to run continually until the power is restored.

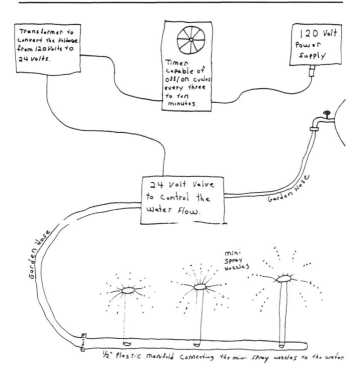

Diagram 7. The above drawing shows how an intermittent mist system is set up. The spray nozzles are very small, yet capable of delivering a fine spray of water in a circular pattern approximately 5 feet in diameter. The spray nozzles are connected to the 1/2" plastic pipe manifold with 3/16" plastic tubing. The manifold is connected to the electric solenoid valve with a piece of heavy duty garden hose. Another piece of heavy duty garden hose connects the solenoid valve to the water supply. The electric timer plugs into a grounded electrical outlet. The primary side of the transformer connects to the timer. The secondary side of the transformer is connected to the electric solenoid valve. As the dial in the timer rotates small levers attached to the dial trip the micro switch every few minutes depending on how many levers you place on the dial. Every time the micro switch is tripped the transformer is energized, thus energizing the electric solenoid valve causing the valve to open and allowing the water to pass through the valve and to the spray nozzles. This flow of water only lasts for a period of about seven seconds. This sequence of events takes place every five minutes or so depending on how often you desire to water your cuttings.

When you take cuttings and prepare them for propagation under intermittent mist, follow the exact same procedures described in the previous section on softwood cuttings.

In northeast Ohio we start our first softwood cuttings around June 1st. If you're in an area further south, you might be able to get started a little earlier.

Another advantage of intermittent mist propagation is if you experience failure with certain cuttings, you can try another batch two or three weeks later. You don't have to wait months to know whether or not you were successful.

The new growth on a landscape plant matures so quickly that a matter of just a few days can make all the difference in the world. One day the cuttings might be too soft to survive, but a few days later the wood will have hardened off to the point that they will do just fine. If you stick some cuttings on June 1st and they are too soft and wilt down immediately, just a few days later the new growth of the very same plant may have hardened off enough to yield cuttings that will do quite well.

Propagation is often hit and miss. Everything we know about plant propagation has been learned through trial and error. The problem is that the people who know all the answers are tight lipped.

The professional propagators in the nursery business spend eight hours a day, fifty two weeks a year, making baby landscape plants, millions and millions of plants. They constantly try new ideas, some of them work and some don't, but just like any other professional in any other industry, they don't give away their trade secrets. Some times it's really funny. I know dozens of people in the nursery business in this area. Many of them are friends. Some are more than willing to share their knowledge, but you won't believe how secretive some of them can be when I ask them how to do something. They just clam up and look at me like I'm from Mars.

I can assure you that writing this book, and making it available to homeowners, is not going to set well with some people in the nursery business. I know they are not going to appreciate me teaching people about mist propagation and selling intermittent mist equipment to homeowners, but I feel that anyone who is willing to put forth the effort to grow their own landscape plants, deserves to have this information.

Intermittent mist was developed primarily to aid in the propagation of softwood cuttings, but I use my mist system from early June through October. In mid September and early October I am still making cuttings and placing them under the mist. As the season progresses and the cuttings require less water, I adjust the system accordingly. By the middle of October I have the system adjusted down to the minimum cycle of a seven second spray every ten minutes. But as the days get shorter I adjust the system to come on later and go off earlier. I just keep reducing the hours of operation until the system is only on 3-4 hours each day.

I made some Rheingold Arborvitae cuttings in mid September last year, and by the time I was closing my nursery up for the winter these cuttings were completely rooted. This was at a time of the year when it is usually too late for softwood cuttings and too early for hardwood cuttings, but by taking advantage of the heat of the sun, and using intermittent mist to keep the cuttings watered lightly, I was able to achieve terrific success.

Chapter Twelve

Growing Plants from Seed

Many landscape plants can be grown from seed, but with so many different plants it is much quicker and easier to grow plants from cuttings than it is to grow them from seed. Seedlings are so tiny and delicate when they first germinate that they require much more care than a cutting.

Many plants will not come true from a seed. In other words, the seedling produced from seeds that were collected from a red Rhododendron are not likely to flower red. More than likely the flowers will be a pale lavender. Seeds collected from a pink Dogwood will most likely flower white.

However, there are certain plants that must be grown from seed. Most Taxus varieties are successfully grown from cuttings, but Taxus Capitata, one of the most attractive varieties of Taxus will not come true from a cutting, but it will come true from seed.

Taxus Capitata is the most popular variety of the pyramidal shaped Taxus. Cuttings from this plant can be rooted and will grow just fine, but the plant will not have the natural pyramidal shape of the parent plant. The plants of this variety grown from cuttings, tend to grow more upright and require much more pruning to obtain the desired pyramidal effect.

Other plants that are routinely grown from seed are plants that are extremely difficult to grow from cuttings. Many ornamental trees either can not be grown from cuttings, or if they are grown from cuttings the plants have weak root systems.

These ornamental trees will not come true from seed, but the plants that are produced from seed have good strong root systems that can be used as rootstock for the desired variety. In this situation the desired variety is grafted on to the healthy, hardy root stock of the seedling. Grafting will be discussed in detail in the next section of this book.

Growing landscape plants from seed is a little more difficult than growing vegetables. The seeds produced by most landscape plants will not germinate until they have under gone certain environmental conditions. Most seeds from landscape plants have a very hard, outer protective shell. Under natural conditions most of these seeds do not receive the proper treatment in order for the seeds to germinate. They just lay on the ground and either dry out or rot.

In different climates, different varieties of plants will grow naturally from seed. In eastern Pennsylvania for instance, Rhododendrons and Mountain Laurel grow wild on the mountain sides. Here in northern Ohio Dogwoods grow wild. Of course only a fraction of the seeds produced in the woods actually make it to the point of germination and survival.

Many seeds go through a period of internal dormancy right after the fruit falls from the tree. In some cases, there is actually a chemical barrier that prevents the seeds from germinating while they are still inside the fruit.

The hard protective coating on some seeds was designed by nature to protect the seed, but in many cases this protective coating actually inhibits the germination of the seed because water and air can not penetrate the hard coating.

Many of these seeds actually require a double dormancy period before they will germinate. In other words, the seeds must lay on the ground completely dormant for one full growing season, and then germinate the following growing season. During the first season the only thing that is taking place is the outer coating is being softened by the elements.

Once the outer coating is softened water and air can penetrate and germination can begin.

Timing is critical. Once the protective coating is softened, and the seeds begin to receive sufficient amounts of oxygen and water to begin germination, the plant will start to grow. However, if this takes place at the wrong time of the year, the young seedling will be destroyed by the intense summer sun, or the freezing temperatures of winter. That's why, of the millions of seeds produced by landscape plants, so few actually germinate and survive to become adult plants.

As a gardener you can control when your seeds will germinate by initiating the pre-treatment and stratification at just the right time. You can actually fool some seeds into germinating much quicker by creating the necessary environmental conditions to soften the outer coating and initiate germination sooner. Let's walk through growing Dogwood trees from seed.

Dogwood seeds ripen in the fall. When the seeds are ripe they will fall to the ground. You can leave them on the ground until they begin to show signs of shriveling. Collect the seeds and place them in a container of water. Allow them to soak a few days to soften the fruit around the actual seed. After soaking for a few days, you should be able to squeeze them with your fingers forcing the seed from the pulp. The good seeds will sink to the bottom of the container of water, any seeds that float are probably not viable. To separate the good seeds from the bad seeds and the pulp, turn your garden hose on very low and stick the end of the hose in the container and fill the container until it very slowly over flows. As the container over flows, the pulp and bad seeds will float out of the container. After a few minutes the only thing left in the bottom of the container will be the good seeds.

Once you have completely separated the seeds from the pulp, mix the seeds with some moist peat moss and place the mixture of peat moss and seeds in a plastic bag. The mixture should be moist, but not too wet. Store the bag at room temperature for a period of 100 days, and then move the bag to your refrigerator for a period of another 100 days.

This process softens the outer coating and allows germination to begin. The first 100 days of this process is a pre-treatment, and the second 100 days is known as stratifying the seeds. After the period of 200 days the seeds can be planted outside in a raised bed, or a flat of 80% peat moss and 20% coarse sand.

Make sure the sand you use is **coarse**. The purpose of the sand is to provide drainage. Sand with fine grains will not provide drainage.

Cover the seeds with a light layer of the growing medium that you are using. The rule of thumb for the correct depth of planting is twice the length of the seed, which is not very deep. If the seeds are 1/8 of an inch in length, they should be planted 1/4 inch deep or less.

Water the seed bed thoroughly after planting, and keep it water throughout the growing season. It is better to water thoroughly and then let the bed dry out, almost completely, before watering again. This allows the sun to warm the soil in between watering. If you water lightly, but more often, you will keep the soil too cool. The seeds need the warmth of the sun as much as they need the water.

You can also speed the germination process by using a knife to make a very small cut or nick in the outer coating of the seed. Make sure you don't damage the interior of the seed. This process allows water and air to enter the seed thus stimulating germination. With the dogwood seeds mentioned above, you could eliminate the first 100 day period of warm storage, by very carefully nicking the seeds, before placing them in the 100 day period of cold storage for stratification.

Cleaned seeds can be stored dry until they have undergone some form or pre-treatment. Just count backwards on your calendar from the day you would like to plant outside. If the seeds you are doing need 100 days of stratification, count backwards 100 days from the day you would like to plant. If they need 100 days of warm storage and another 100 days of cold storage, count backwards 200 days.

Another pre-treating technique often used, is treating the seeds with almost boiling water before storing them at a cool temperature. For instance, this technique is often used for Japanese Maple seeds.

Just place the seeds in a Styrofoam cup and fill the cup with extremely hot water, but not quite hot enough to boil. Allow the seeds to soak in this water as it cools overnight. Remove the seeds from the cup and place them in a plastic bag with the peat moss mixture as mentioned earlier, and store them in the refrigerator for a period of 90-120 days.

This process helps to soften the outer coating and eliminates storing them at room temperature for 100 days.

Seeds with a hard outer coating need one of the pre-treatments mentioned here, prior to the stratification period. One of the pre-treatments must be done prior to the stratification period.

When planting seeds outside in the spring you should wait until after the danger of frost has passed before sowing the seeds. Here in northern Ohio it is best to wait until after May 15th to be safe. You should count backwards on your calendar from the planting date, so you know when to start stratifying the seeds. With different kinds of seeds, and seeds from different plants, the length of time it takes to stratify the seeds can vary considerably. Sometimes only trial and error will provide you with the correct stratification period for seeds from a specific plant.

Check your seeds at least once a week when you are stratifying them. Make sure they are not too wet, and if they need water give them a little drink. They should be moist, but not wet. If they are too wet, squeeze some of the water out. The bag should be closed but not sealed completely air tight. If you notice that 10% or more of the seeds have started to sprout, plant them right away. If it is not practical to plant them outside, sow them in flats indoors, and make sure they receive some light. If you see mold growing in the bag, apply a powder fungicide.

Rhododendron and Azalea seeds ripen in the early fall. The best time to collect them is when the capsules darken, before they begin to open. If you wait too long, they will be blown away by the wind. These seeds can be kept in a dry place at room temperature until spring planting, or you can plant them right, away if you can keep them at about 70 degrees F.. Just sow them on top of a flat filled with a mixture of peat moss and coarse sand, and provide them with some light. Use a mixture of 20% sand and 80% peat moss.

When growing seeds outdoors it is helpful to build a wooden frame and fill it with a mixture of peat moss and sand. Use a mixture of 20% sand and 80% peat moss. This will make it easier for you to control the moisture, and will also help to reduce weed growth. Topsoil is much more nutritional than peat moss, but unless the topsoil has been sterilized, it is likely to contain millions of weed seeds.

Some growers cover their seed beds with clear plastic as soon as they sow the seeds in the spring. This helps to warm the soil, and to retain the moisture. As soon as the seedlings begin to grow, the plastic is removed and some type of shading is provided. Snow fence suspended over the seed bed provides about 50% shade which is adequate.

Pines, spruce and firs are grown from seed. The pine cones are collected in the fall just before they open. Place them in a paper bag so when they open the seeds don't get blown away. Store them in a cool dry place and plant them in a flat or a seed bed in the spring.

Most varieties of Hemlock require a stratification period of 30 days, in moist peat, in the refrigerator. The rule of thumb for determining how much peat moss to mix with the seeds, is four times the volume of the seeds.

Some seeds germinate immediately after falling from the tree. Most varieties of Oak trees fall into this category. For specific information on each variety see the **"How to Do What"** section in the back of the book.

Chapter 13

Grafting

Grafting is one of the most interesting forms of plant propagation. It is also one of the most tedious and least used forms of propagation. Many wholesale nurserymen stay away from grafting because it is just too labor intensive. They either will not grow plants that have to be grafted, or they will buy small grafted plants from someone who specializes in grafting. Don't let that scare you off. Nurserymen are in business to make money. If it takes too long to produce a particular plant, they just stay away from it. They feel that they can do much better financially, growing something easier to produce. If you are daring enough to try your hand at grafting, you will realize a tremendous amount of pride and self satisfaction. Grafting is not difficult, it just takes patience.

One of the most beautiful landscape plants on this planet is the Laceleaf Weeping Japanese Red Maple. This tree is very low growing, most are not more than 4' tall. The branches spread out, making the tree wider than it is tall. The branches weep from the top of the tree to the ground, the foliage is deep red in color and the leaves are delicately cut on the edges. This plant is breath taking during the spring and summer months. Nobody walks by this plant without taking notice. It is just as interesting during the winter, the weeping branches create a very unique effect even though the plant is without leaves.

The only method of propagation for the Laceleaf Weeping Japanese Red Maple is grafting. Very few nurseries grow them. That's why a 3' tall plant in a garden center is likely to have a price tag of $150.00 or more. You can grow one yourself for a little bit of nothing.

Grafting is the art of attaching a piece of one plant to another in such a way that the two pieces will bond and become one plant. One plant is used to provide the root system and sometimes the stem, while the other plant is grafted on to this plant to grow into the variety of plant the grower actually desires.

In the case of the Laceleaf Weeping Japanese Red Maple, the root stock would be a Japanese Maple grown from seed. The Laceleaf Weeping Japanese Red Maple would be the desired variety. A small piece of this desired variety would be grafted on to the rootstock to create the desired plant.

If you would like to create a Laceleaf

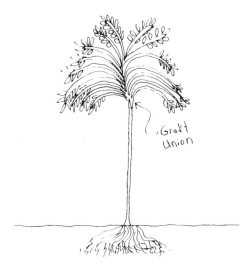

Diagram 8. **The above drawing shows a grafted weeping plant that has been grafted much higher than the soil level. Some plants are done this way and some are grafted right at the soil level so the graft union does not show. In this case everything shown below the graft union is that of the root stock (A Japanese Maple seedling.), and everything above the graft union is that of the desired variety.**

Weeping Japanese Maple through the magic of grafting, you must first raise a regular Japanese Maple tree from seed to use as the rootstock. You can do this using the techniques described in the section of growing landscape plants from seed.

Japanese Maple seeds have a hard seed coat and can be pre-treated by soaking in hot water as described in the previous section of this book. After pre-treating store them in a bag of moist peat in the refrigerator for a period of 100-120 days before planting. This procedure should induce germination and the seedlings will start growing shortly after planting them out.

If your seedlings come up quite close together, they should be transplanted where they will have more room, this can be done either in the late fall or early spring. Allow the seedlings to grow until they are about 3/16" to 1/4" in diameter.

Grafting of this nature should be done in January or February. In the late fall pot up the seedlings that you intend to use as rootstock for grafting that winter. (*Use a good quality, well drained, bagged potting soil.*) Keep these potted plants outside, but in a protected area until about January 15th. Make sure they do not dry out. Plants need moisture during the winter as well as during the growing season. You must leave them outside, so they remain dormant up until the time you are ready to use them.

You can build a wooden frame and cover it with white plastic for protection. White plastic reflects the sun. Don't use clear plastic, it will get too warm inside when the sun is out, the plants will start to break dormancy, and then sustain damage when the temperature dips below freezing at night. When storing plants for the winter you want them to stay at one constant temperature.

COLOR BELT TESTING

Bellevue School –Friday, April 3rd– 7:00 PM
Cranberry School – Saturday, April 4th– 10:00 AM

Butler School – Saturday, April 4th– 1:30 PM

Main School – Saturday, April 11th- 10:00 AM

Fox Chapel School – Saturday ,April 11th- 1:30 PM

Make-up Testing at the Main School
Friday, April 17th 7:30 PM

Gibsonia School – Saturday, April 25th- 10:00 AM

Mercer School – Saturday, April 25th– 3:30 PM

Colored Belt Testing Fees: $55.00
Late Fee: $10.00 additional

FORMS ARE LATE IF THEY ARE NOT TURNED IN AT LEAST THREE DAYS PRIOR TO *YOUR SCHOOL'S* SCHEDULED TEST.

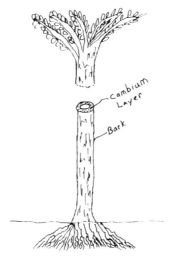

Diagram 9. This is a drawing of the stem and roots of a tree, the top of the tree has been cut off to show a cross section of the inside of the tree. As we all know the outside of the tree is the tree bark. The very inside of the tree is the wood. The thin layer between the bark and the wood is the cambium layer. The cambium layer is the life support system for the tree, all of the water, food, and nutrients are delivered from the root system to the top of the tree via the cambium layer. When you are grafting you must match up the cambium layer of the rootstock and the cambium layer of the scion in order for the graft to be successful.

Once you bring them inside, you should let them warm up for a period of 2-3 weeks before you start grafting. Keep them at temperature of 70 degrees F. After about 14 days the plants should start showing signs that they are beginning to break dormancy. At this point they should be grafted immediately. The piece of the desired variety that is to be grafted onto the rootstock should remain outdoors in the cold (*completely dormant*) right up until the day you are going to graft. You don't want this part of the plant trying to grow until the graft is at

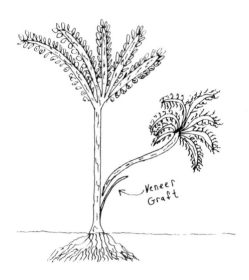

Veneer Graft

Diagram 10. This is an example of veneer grafting. The larger plant is the rootstock. The small branch on the right is the desired variety, known as the scion. A small slice is made into the rootstock just below the bark, into the cambium layer. The scion is cut to a taper on the end, exposing the cambium layer of the scion. The scion is slid down into the crotch of the cut, making sure the cambium layers of both pieces match up tightly. Once in place the flap from the rootstock is pressed tightly against the scion and a rubber band is wrapped around the union holding it tight until the graft is completely healed. A layer of melted grafting wax is applied with a brush to keep the graft union air tight.

least partially healed.

In order to achieve success with grafting you need to understand exactly what part of the plants you must bond together. There is a thin layer of tissue sandwiched between the bark of the tree and the wood, this tissue is known as the cambium layer.

You might liken the cambium layer of a tree to the circulatory system in your own body. The cambium layer transfers water and nutrients to the top of the plant from the roots and vice versa.

When grafting it is extremely important that you bond the cambium layer of the rootstock with the cambium layer of the scion. (*The scion is the term used to describe the piece of the desired plant variety that you are attaching to the rootstock.*) Matching up these two surfaces as closely as possible is extremely important. These two sections of cambium layer are going to bond and will be the only thing holding the plant together. This bond is almost like a natural form of welding.

There are many different kinds of grafts, but all are based on the same basic theory. Match up two compatible plants and bond the two cambium layers together.

Performing the actual task of making the graft union is not that difficult. The secret is to make sure that as you cut into the cambium layer, you do not cut too deeply, and into the wood. Make sure the scion wood and the rootstock are as close to the same size diameter as possible. If they are different sizes, the cambium layers will not line up and the grafts will

Diagram 11. This is a saddle graft. The rootstock has been cut to a taper and the scion is split in such a way that it can sit on top of the rootstock. Having both scion and rootstock of the same size diameter is extremely important when doing this type of graft.

not be successful. *(In my video tape "How to Grow Your Own Landscape Plants From Scratch", you can watch me doing some actual grafting. If you are interested in the video, there is ordering information in the back of this book.)*

Once you have joined the plants together the graft union should be wrapped with a rubber band to firmly hold the twigs in place. After the rubber band is in place the entire graft union should be coated with melted grafting wax to keep the union air tight. If air gets into the graft union the cambium layers will dry out and not bond. Make sure the grafting wax is not too hot. Just warm enough for it to melt is as hot as you should let it get. If the wax is too hot tissue damage can occur. The rubber band should be left on for a period of about 8 weeks.

Caring for your recently grafted plants after the process is complete is extremely important to the success of your efforts. Once the graft is complete keep the plants warm, 70 degrees F. is ideal.
Maintain this temperature for a period of at least three to four weeks, giving the graft unions plenty of time to heal.

Maintaining a relatively high humidity around the graft union also helps the healing process. One way to do this is to wrap the graft union with a piece of plastic cellophane and make sure some moisture gets trapped under the plastic.
Make sure your plants also receive some light. Natural light from a window is best, but if that is not possible provide some artificial light.

Don't move your new grafts outside until the danger of frost has past. Be careful not to put them in the full sun right away. At least 50% shade is best until they harden off completely. I keep my grafted plants under shade for the entire first season. I also provide winter protection for them during their first winter outside.

Grafting is not difficult to do, but it does require patience and an area where you can work

Photograph 6. This is a recently grafted Laceleaf Weeping Japanese Red Maple. This is a veneer graft. I grafted this plant in February and took this photo in September. One of the advantages of veneer grafting is that you are attaching the scion to the side of the rootstock, so you do not have to remove the top of the rootstock until the graft has successfully bonded. This allows the rootstock to continue to grow which helps support the graft as it heals. Looking at the photo you can see on the right where I cut off the top of the rootstock just above the graft union. You can also see some left over grafting wax. This graft union is not very attractive, but as the tree grows the weeping canopy will come down over the graft union, and it will not be visible.

require patience and an area where you can work indoors during the winter. It is well worth the time and effort you put into. Grafting can produce some of the most unique plants for a home landscape.

Chapter Fourteen

Budding

Budding is another form of grafting, except with budding you do not attach a small branch of the desired variety, you only insert a single bud under the bark of the rootstock.

Budding is a mid to late summer project, usually around the end of July or the beginning of August. It is at this time of the year that the bark of the young trees will slip. In other words, the bark is somewhat loose from the tree and a bud can be slipped between the bark and the cambium layer.

Budding is easier than grafting and is used quite often in the nursery industry. Almost all flowering crab apples are propagated through the budding process.

The rootstock is grown from seed using the techniques described earlier. Once the rootstock reaches 1/4" in diameter, the budding is done. A small 'T' shaped cut is made in the bark of the rootstock, the bark is gently pulled away from the cambium layer with a knife, but only enough to allow a single bud to be slipped under the bark.

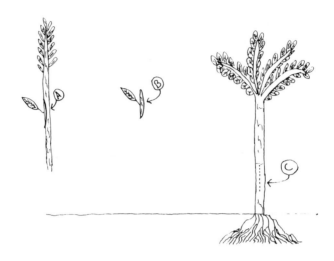

Diagram 12. Sketch 'A' shows the bud still attached to the branch of the desired plant variety. Sketch 'B' shows the how the bud is removed from the parent plant. Notice the bud is attached to a piece of bark with some cambium tissue also. Sketch 'C' indicates how the 'T" shaped cut should be made into the bark of the rootstock. After the cut is made the bark should be pulled back slightly so the piece of bark and cambium can be slipped under the bark. The bud itself should protrude through the cut in the bark of the rootstock. A rubber band is then wrapped around the rootstock pulling the bark tight so the two pieces can heal, and bond together. The following spring the rootstock should be cut off just above the bud. The bud will grow and eventually mature into a tree identical to the parent plant.

The bud you are going to insert under the bark of the rootstock will be removed from a branch of the variety you would like to grow. You can remove a small branch from the desired variety. This branch is called a bud stick. This bud stick can have as many as 20 or more usable buds on it. Each bud has a leaf attached to it. Pinch the leaf off but leave the leaf stem, this stem will serve as a handle as you work with the bud. If you have 100 different crabapple rootstocks that you grew from seed, you can grow many different varieties of flowering crabapples by inserting different varieties of buds into these rootstocks.

After you have made the "T" cut in the rootstock and loosened the bark slightly, you are ready to remove the desired bud from the bud stick. The bud is removed by slicing into the branch under the bud you are removing. Almost like peeling an apple, except you cut below the bark and remove a piece of bark along with the cambium layer attached. The bud is still attached to the piece of bark and cambium you remove. Do this carefully and do not cut into the bud and damage it. By the same token, you don't want to cut too deeply into the wood, just below the cambium layer is good. See chapter 13 to learn more about the cambium layer.

As soon as the bud is removed from the parent plant it should be immediately inserted under the bark of the rootstock. Once inserted, the bud union should be wrapped securely with a rubber band so the bonding process can begin. Nothing further should be done this growing season. Just let Mother Nature take over until spring.

Early in the spring, while the plant is still dormant, the rootstock should be cut off just above the inserted bud. When the plant breaks dormancy the bud will begin to grow into a plant identical to the parent plant.

Budding is a much simpler form of grafting because you can do it during the summer months and do not have to provide artificial heat, or protection for the plant over the winter months. Budding does not work for all plants, but it is used on a wide variety of fruit trees and crab apples.

It can also be used to create the Weeping Cotoneaster tree I describe on page 8. Many Weeping Cherries are also grown through the budding process.

Chapter Fifteen

How to Do What

Arborvitae: Cuttings taken in mid to late summer can be rooted in coarse sand under intermittent mist. Cuttings taken in the fall can be rooted in coarse sand in an outdoor frame. Cuttings taken during the winter can be rooted in coarse sand with bottom heat.

Ash Trees: Collect the seeds when they ripen and plant them out right away. Most should germinate the first season.

Azaleas, deciduous varieties: Most deciduous Azaleas are grown from seeds collected in the fall and planted immediately. I would sow them in a flat, in an area where they can be kept warm and receive some natural or artificial light. You can also try softwood cuttings, preferably under intermittent mist.

Azaleas, evergreen: Most growers do evergreen Azaleas in the late fall with bottom heat. You can try softwood cuttings around June 1st.

Barberry: Most varieties of Barberry can be done by either softwood cuttings in early June, or hardwood cuttings in the late fall.

Boston Ivy: Grow from seed. Plant outdoors in late April or early May.

European Beech: Grow from seed. Collect when ripe, plant outdoors immediately.

Purple Leaf Weeping Beech: This variety must be grafted on to a Beech variety grown from seed.

White Birch: Grow from seed. Collect the seeds when ripe and plant outdoors in the fall.

Weeping White Birch: This variety must be grafted on to a Birch rootstock grown from seed.

Boxwood: Softwood cuttings in July under intermittent mist or hardwood cuttings in mid to late fall in and outdoor frame. Winter cuttings with bottom heat.

Burning Bush: Softwood cuttings in late May or early June, hardwood cuttings in late mid to late fall in an outdoor frame.

Weeping Cherries: Weeping cherries must be grafted on to a cherry rootstock grown from seed. Collect the seeds when ripe, stratify 150 days over winter, plant in the spring. I have also had some success with softwood cuttings under intermittent mist.

Blue False Cypress: Semi-hardwood cuttings in late August under intermittent mist, or hardwood cuttings in the late fall with bottom heat.

Gold Thread Cypress: Hardwood cuttings in late fall with bottom heat. You can try some semi-hardwood cuttings in late summer under intermittent mist.

Clematis: Softwood cuttings in late spring. As with almost all softwood cuttings, intermittent mist will dramatically increase your success.

Cotoneaster: Softwood cuttings in early June, or hardwood cuttings in late fall.

Flowering Crabapples: Most varieties of flowering Crabapple must be grafted or budded on to a rootstock grown from seed. Collect the seeds as they ripen in the fall and plant them outdoors immediately.

Daylilies: Propagate by division in the fall or the spring.

Chinese Dogwood: Softwood cuttings in early June or grow from seed. Collect the seed in the fall when ripe. Stratify in moist peat at room temperature for 100 days, and then in your refrigerator for another 100 days, then plant outside.

Pink Dogwood: Softwood   cuttings   under intermittent mist in early June, or bud or graft on to a white dogwood seedling.

Red Twig Dogwood: Layering in April or May, or softwood cuttings in June, or hardwood cuttings in late fall.

Yellow Twig Dogwood: Layering in April or May, or softwood cuttings in June, or hardwood cuttings in late fall.

Variegated Dogwood Trees: Softwood cuttings under intermittent mist in early June, or bud or graft on to a white dogwood seedling.

White Dogwood: Softwood cuttings in early June or grow from seed. Collect the seed in the fall when ripe. Stratify in moist peat at room temperature for 100 days, and then in your refrigerator for another 100 days, then plant outside.

English Ivy: Softwood cuttings during the summer beginning in early June.

Variegated Euonymus Varieties: Softwood cuttings beginning in June. Hardwood cuttings in the fall outside in a frame of course sand.

Firethorne (Pyracantha): Softwood cuttings in June, or semi-hardwood cuttings in the fall in a frame of course sand.

Fir, Concolor: Grow from seed. Collect the seeds in the fall and store them in a cool dry place until spring. Sow the seeds outdoors in the spring. Cover the seed bed with clear plastic until the seeds begin to germinate.

Forsythia: Layering in spring or fall, softwood cuttings in June, hardwood cuttings in the late fall or winter.

Washington Hawthorn: Grow from seed. Collect the seeds in the fall and plant them in an outdoor seed bed immediately.

Canadian Hemlock: Grow from seed. Collect the pine cones in the fall before they open and release the seeds into the air. Place the pine cones in a paper bag to catch the seeds as the cones open. Store the seeds in a cool dry place until spring, stratify for 30 days in moist peat in your refrigerator, and plant outside after the danger of frost has passed.

English Holly: Hardwood cuttings, late fall with bottom heat.

Japanese Holly: Medium softwood cuttings in mid summer, or hardwood cuttings in the fall in and outside frame of sand. Or hardwood cuttings in late fall or winter with bottom heat.

Honeysuckle: Layering in the spring, softwood cuttings in early June, or hardwood cuttings in the fall.

Hosta: Propagate by dividing in late fall or early spring.

Blue Hydrangea: Softwood cuttings, or division.

P.G. Hydrangea: Layering in the spring, or softwood cuttings in early June.

Junipers: Softwood to semi-hardwood cuttings in mid to late summer under intermittent mist, hardwood cuttings in the fall in an outdoor frame, or hardwood cuttings in late fall or winter with bottom heat.

Leucothoe: Softwood cuttings in June or hardwood cuttings in the fall.

Lilacs: Lilacs must be budded or grafted on to a rootstock grown from seed. Either a lilac seedling or some growers use privet as a rootstock.

Linden Trees: Grow from seed. Collect the seeds when ripe and plant immediately.

Lirope: Propagate by division.

Magnolia: Some varieties are grown from seed, and others are budded on to these seedlings.

Maple Trees: Grow from seed. Collect the seeds when ripe and plant immediately.

Japanese Maple: Grow from seed. Collect the seeds when ripe and store until late fall. Pre-treat the seeds by soaking overnight in hot water, and then stratify in moist peat for 90-120 days in your refrigerator. Then plant them outside.

Weeping Japanese Maple: This variety must be grafted on to a rootstock grown from seed.

Mockorange: Layering in the spring, softwood cuttings in June, and hardwood cuttings in the fall and winter.

Mountain Ash Trees: Grow from seed. Collect when ripe and plant immediately.

Blue Myrtle: Propagate by division.

Oak Trees: Grow from seed. Collect when ripe and plant immediately.

Ornamental Grasses: Propagate by division.

Pachysandra: Propagate by division, or softwood cuttings.

Bradford Pear Trees: Grow from seed. Collect when ripe and stratify in moist peat in your refrigerator for 60-90 days.

Flowering Plum Trees: Desired varieties must be budded on to a rootstock grown from seed. Collect the seeds when ripe and stratify in moist peat in your refrigerator for 150 days before planting outside.

White Pine Trees: Grow from seed. Collect the pine cones in the fall before they open and allow them to open in a paper bag to catch the seeds. Store in a cool dry place until spring, then sow them outside.

Weeping White Pine: Must be grafted on to a white

pine seedling.

Austrian Pine: Grow from seed. Collect the pine cones in the fall before they open and allow them to open in a paper bag to catch the seeds. Store in a cool dry place until spring, then sow them outside.

Mugho Pine: Grow from seed. Plant them outside in the spring.

Potentilla: Softwood cuttings in June, or hardwood cuttings in the late fall.

Poplar Trees: Grow from seed. Collect the seeds when ripe and plant outside immediately. Also softwood cuttings or hardwood cuttings.

Purple Leaf Winter Creeper: Softwood cuttings in early June, or semi-hardwood cuttings throughout the summer.

Pussy Willow: Layering in the spring, softwood cuttings in early June, or hardwood cuttings in the late fall.

Privet: Layering in the spring, softwood cuttings in early June, or hardwood cuttings in the late fall.

Red Bud Trees: Grow from seed. Collect when ripe

and plant outside in the spring.

Rhododendrons: Can be grown from seed. Collect in the fall and grow in a flat, indoors at 70 degrees F. with some light. Hybrid varieties must be grown from cuttings. Softwoods in early June under intermittent mist, or hardwoods in perlite peat moss mixture in the late fall with bottom heat.

Rose of Sharon: Layering in the spring, softwood cuttings in early June, or hardwood cuttings in the late fall.

Purple Sandcherry: Layering in the spring, softwood cuttings in early June, or hardwood cuttings in the late fall.

Spiraea: Layering in the spring, softwood cuttings in early June, or hardwood cuttings in the late fall.

Dwarf Alberta Spruce: Softwood cuttings in mid to late June under intermittent mist, or hardwood cuttings in the late fall with bottom heat.

Colorado Blue Spruce: Grow from seed. Collect the pine cones in the fall before they open and allow them to open in a paper bag to catch the seeds. Store in a cool dry place until spring, then sow them outside.

Viburnum: Layering in the spring, softwood cuttings in early June, or hardwood cuttings in the late fall.

Weigela: Layering in the spring, softwood cuttings in early June, or hardwood cuttings in the late fall.

Wisteria: Layering in the spring, softwood cuttings in early June, or hardwood cuttings in the late fall.

Weeping Willow: Layering in the spring, softwood cuttings in early June, or hardwood cuttings in the late fall.

Witch Hazel: Layering in the spring, softwood cuttings in early June, or hardwood cuttings in the late fall.

Yews (Taxus): Softwood cuttings in early July through early August, or hardwood cuttings in the fall in course sand in an outside frame, or hardwood cuttings in late fall or winter with bottom heat.

Yucca: Propagate by taking cuttings from the roots in early spring and planting outside. Just cut a piece of root about 3/4" long and plant it below the surface of the soil about 1/2".

Don't forget to check out the back of the book for more interesting landscape gardening offers.

Chapter Sixteen

What You Should Be Doing Now

January:

You can do hardwood cuttings of deciduous plants. Just wait for a day when the ground is not frozen so you can either plant them out, or bury them as described in the section on hardwood cuttings.

You can also do hardwood cuttings of evergreens, if you can provide them with some bottom heat.

If you are going to do any grafting, now is the time to bring in your rootstock and let them warm up so they can begin to break dormancy.

February:

You can still do hardwood cuttings as described for January. Start your grafting toward the middle or end of the month.

March:

It's a little late for hardwood cuttings of evergreens, but you can still do some hardwood cuttings of deciduous plants. As soon as the ground thaws and spring begins to peak around the corner you can start doing plants that can be propagated by division. You can also start to do some layering.

If you have landscape plants that need pruning, do it now before they begin to grow. Any transplanting that you intend to do should be done now before the plants break dormancy.

April:

There are plenty of things to do in April. You can still do some division as long as the plants are not too far out of dormancy. You can do layering, air layering and serpentine layering. If you have seeds that you have been stratifying, you can plant them out as long as they have been in stratification for the proper length of time.

April is also the time to start thinking about an intermittent mist system. Don't wait until the last minute to order the equipment. You want to be all ready to go when the cuttings are ready to be taken. There is information on ordering a "Plant Magic" mist system in the back of the book.

May:

You can continue all methods of layering. All seeds should now be ready to plant out. You can also collect seeds that ripen in the spring. By the end of the month you should be able to start some softwood cuttings, unless you are in a northern state.

June:

By now you should be able to do softwood cuttings of just about all deciduous plants. If you are going to do softwood cuttings of Rhododendrons, try some early in June. If they don't do well, try a few more later in the month. If you are using intermittent mist you can experiment with all kinds of different plants. June is a little early to be doing softwood cuttings of evergreens but you can test a few.

July:

Continue with softwood cuttings of deciduous plants. Now is the time to start some softwood cuttings of evergreens. By mid to late July you can start budding dogwoods, apples, crab apples, cherries, and anything else you would like to bud.

August:

Continue with softwood cuttings of evergreens. By now the wood of most deciduous plants has hardened off. You can still make cuttings with this harder wood if you are using intermittent mist, but you should use a little stronger concentration of rooting compound. Budding can be done early in August.

September:

Start watching for fall seeds to ripen and start collecting them. Evergreen cuttings can still be taken and rooted under intermittent mist. If you are not using mist you can stick them in a bed of sand and keep them watered.

October:

Hardwood cuttings of evergreens can be stuck in a bed of sand. Or you can start sticking hardwood cuttings of evergreens using bottom heat. After a good hard frost you can start dividing perennials. Collect pines cones from Pines, Spruce, and Firs, as the cones open they release the seeds inside. Store the seeds in a cool dry place until spring for plantings. Seed pods from Rhododendrons and Deciduous Azaleas can also be collected.

November:

Hardwood cuttings of evergreens can be stuck either in a bed of sand outdoors or indoors with bottom heat. Hardwood cuttings of deciduous plants can be done by either of the methods mentioned in the section on hardwood cuttings.

If you intend to do some grafting over the winter, now is the time to make sure your rootstock is potted up and placed in a protected, but cold area until January.

December:

You can do hardwood cuttings of evergreens in a bed of sand or with bottom heat. You can also do hardwood cuttings of deciduous plants as long as the ground is not frozen.

Index

100
Purple leaf winter creeper, 107
Purple sandcherry, 63,108
Pussy willow, 107
Pyracantha, 103
Raised beds, 15,17,80
Red bud trees, 108
Red twig dogwood, 102
Refrigeration, 82
Registered trademarks, 6
Rheingold Arborvitae, 74
Rhododendrons, 8, 23,25,29,45,64,108
Root activity, 27
Root development, 30,40,51
Rooting inducing compound, 31,40
Rooting process, 46
Rootstock, 10,86,95
Root systems, 76
Rose of sharon, 108
Rubber bands, 88, 90
Sand 55
Saddle graft, 92
Sandy soil, 15
Scion, 90,91
Seeds, 75
Seedlings, 75,88,
Semi softwood cuttings,
Serpentine layering, 34
Shade, 42,84
Shrubs, 15
Small plants, 32

Snow cover, 36
Snow fence, 84
Softwood cuttings, 33,37,38,65,67
Softwood cuttings of deciduous plants, 37
Softwood cuttings of evergreens, 45
Soil temperatures, 27,32,60,62
Solenoid valve, 69
Spiraea, 108
Spray nozzles, 69
Spruce, 84
Standing water, 56
Steel hoops, 57
Stock plants, 33
Storing plants, 89
Stratification, 79
Taxus, 45, 109
Taxus capitata, 75
Taxus varieties, 75
Temperatures, 36
Terminal buds, 20
Thermostats, 60, 62
Timers, 66
Time to prune, 21
Tip cuttings, 40
Topsoil, 83
Transformer, 69,71
Transplanting, 27,53
Trees, 15
Variegated dogwood trees, 102
Variegated euonymus, 11,103

You can keep in touch with the author of this book by subscribing to his newsletter

"Grow'n Your Own Landscape Plants, Plus Landscaping Magic"

You will learn new techniques to help you achieve greater landscape gardening success. Including new plant starting techniques. You will also learn countless landscaping techniques and ideas. From time to time you will receive simple, yet beautiful landscape designs that can be adapted to any home. You will be made aware of what pests to look for on your landscape plants, and how to treat them, and prevent them.   Sample copies are only $1.00, and a One Year Subscription is only $6.00. (Ohio residents add 35 cents sales tax.)
$8.00 for Canadian subscribers, and $14.00 for all other countries. Published four times a year.

Send your order to:
"Grow'n Your Own Landscape Plants, Plus Landscaping Magic"
4390 Middle Ridge Rd.
Perry, Ohio 44081

Hey Mike, Sign me up! Enclosed is my check or money order in the amount of $6.00. Please start my subscription to "Grow'n Your Own Landscape Plants, Plus Landscaping Magic" as soon as possible.

Name _____

Address _____

City_____ State _____ Zip _____

Must Sell!!!

Surplus landscape plants as low as 89 cents each!

At the **"McGroarty Family Nursery"** we often produce more landscape plants than we have room for. Our nursery is actually quite small, just a backyard operation, and we currently are not interested in expanding. So we offer our surplus plants to our friends who have purchased the book, **"Free Landscape Plants"**, or subscribe to our quarterly newsletter. (only $6.00 per year!)

As surplus plants become available, a list of these plants is mailed with the newsletter. Or you can obtain a copy by sending a self-addressed, stamped envelope to:

"Surplus Landscape Plants"
The McGroarty Family Nursery
4390 Middle Ridge Rd.
Perry, Ohio 44081

Now on Video!

"How to Grow Your Own Landscape Plants From Scratch"

There is nothing like video for learning new skills. This video was produced at **"The McGroarty Family Nursery"**. This video includes a variety of landscape plant propagation techniques. You will learn how to start plants through techniques such as; layering, softwood cuttings, hardwood cuttings, intermittent mist, growing plants from seed, and grafting. Approximately one hour and fifty minutes in length. Order your copy today! It's only $24.95 plus $2.00 shipping and handling. (Ohio residents add $1.44 sale tax.) **One Year Money Back Guarantee**

Canadian customers send $29.95.
Other foreign customers $39.95.
(Only available is VHS format.)

Send your order to:
The McGroarty Family Nursery
4390 Middle Ridge Rd.
Perry, Ohio 44081

- -

Please send me the video tape **"How to Grow Your Own Landscape Plants From Scratch"**. I am enclosing $26.95. ($24.95 plus $2.00 shipping and handling. Ohio residents add $1.44 sales tax.)

Name _____

Address _____

City _____ State ____ Zip _____

You can learn how to design a beautiful landscape for your home.

Designing a beautiful landscape is as easy as 1-2-3 once you learn the basic techniques of landscape design. Over a period of twenty years Michael McGroarty has designed beautiful residential landscapes for hundreds of delighted customers.

You can learn Mike's most closely guarded landscape design techniques. Mike has produced an informative "how to" video tape. You will learn what plants to use, and how and where to use them. You will learn which plants best compliment each other, and how to arrange plants to obtain the ultimate in contrast and continuity. You will learn how to prepare and layout the beds, and how to plant so the plants thrive. **"How to Design a Beautiful landscape for Your Home"** is approximately one hour and 50 minutes in length. Order your copy today! It's only $24.95, plus $2.00 shipping and handling. Send your order to:

Canadian customers send $29.95. Other foreign customers $39.95. (Only available is VHS format.)

The McGroarty Family Nursery
4390 Middle Ridge Rd.
Perry, Ohio 44081

Please send me the video **"How to Design a Beautiful landscape for Your Home"**. I understand that I must be absolutely, positively 100% satisfied or I can return the video anytime within the next twelve months for a full and prompt refund. On those conditions I am enclosing $24.95 plus $2.00 shipping and handling. (Ohio residents please enclose $1.44 sales tax) **One Year Money Back Guarantee!**

Name————————————————————————

Address ——————————————————————

City——————————— State———— Zip——————

You can set up an intermittent mist system in your backyard.

Intermittent mist is by far the simplest, easiest, and quickest way there is to root cuttings of landscape plants.

Intermittent mist allows you to root cuttings during the summer when most other techniques produce mediocre results at best. Many varieties can be rooted in just a few weeks time using intermittent mist.

Intermittent mist is the system used by wholesale nurseries all over the world, because it works great!

I have put together a complete mist system for the home gardener. This is the same equipment I use in my backyard nursery. This system is ready to go!

All you have to do is hook it up to a garden hose, and plug the controls into an electrical outlet. In a matter of minutes your cuttings can be well on their way to establishing roots under the care of one of the most effective systems in the world.

This system comes with three spray nozzles. Each nozzle sprays a fine mist in a circular pattern approx. 5' in diameter. You can set the timer for a 5 to 15 second spray as often as you need it. Once, twice, or three times in a ten minute period.

This system is adequate for a bed 4' by 8'. In this size area you can root several thousand cuttings at one time. By simply adding three more spray nozzles you can double the number of cuttings you can root. Order your **Plant Magic Mist System** today! It's only $349.00 plus $10.00 shipping and handling.

Mike, please rush me a **Plant Magic Mist System** as soon as possible. Enclosed is $359.00.

Name_____

Address_____

City_____

State_____Zip_____

Plant Magic Mist System
4390 Middle Ridge Rd.
Perry, Ohio 44081

You know somebody who would love to have a copy of this book

Do them a favor. Surprise your friends. You can order a copy for a friend, or several copies for several friends. We will ship the book or books directly to your friends along with a note telling them the book is from you, and how lucky they are to have you as a friend.

This book makes an excellent gift. A gift that a gardening enthusiast will cherish for many years to come.

To order for your friends just send $11.95 per book and the names and shipping addresses for each book. Be sure to include your name so we can tell them the book is from you. Just clearly print or type all of the information on a piece of paper and mail to the address below.

Save $1.00 per book!

Order 3 books or more and pay only $10.95 per book.

Canadian customers send $13.95 per book, other foreign customers $15.95 per book. Thanks for the order !-Mike

Send your order to:

The McGroarty Family Nursery
4390 Middle Ridge Rd.
Perry, Ohio 44081

The Laceleaf, Weeping, Japanese Red Maple

In my opinion, this is the most beautiful and elegant landscape plant on this planet. (This photo does not do it justice.) The brilliant red and delicately cut foliage is breath taking. No landscape should be without this wonderful tree. The weeping habit makes it truly a dwarf tree that is likely to grow wider than it does tall. Hardy to zone 5, this plant is an asset to any landscape. Often selling for $150. to $300. in garden centers. Here at the McGroarty Family Nursery we have a few at only $59.00 each, while the supply lasts.

I am enclosing $59.00 plus $8.00 shipping and packing for a total of $67.00, please rush me one of your beautiful Laceleaf, Weeping Japanese Red Maples as soon as possible. (Ohio residents add $3.39 sales tax.) Send your order to: The McGroarty Family Nursery
    4390 Middle Ridge Rd.
    Perry, Ohio 44081

Name _____

Address _____

City _____ State _____ Zip _____